THE DIVINE
KUMBH

THE DIVINE KUMBH

Echoes of Eternity: Ganga, Shipra, Godavari, and Sangam

DEEPAK KUMAR SEN

NIYOGI
BOOKS

Published by
NIYOGI BOOKS
Block D, Building No. 77,
Okhla Industrial Area, Phase-I,
New Delhi-110 020, INDIA
Tel: 011-26818960, +91 7428978881
Email: niyogibooks@gmail.com
Website: www.niyogibooksindia.com

Text © Deepak Kumar Sen
Photos © Deepak Kumar Sen & Abhimanyu Sharma

Editor: Anwesha Panda
Design: Shashi Bhushan Prasad

ISBN: 978-81-19626-26-7
Publication: 2024

Printed at Niyogi Offset Pvt. Ltd., New Delhi, India

In memory of
Sir J.K. Sen (1937–2021)

Contents

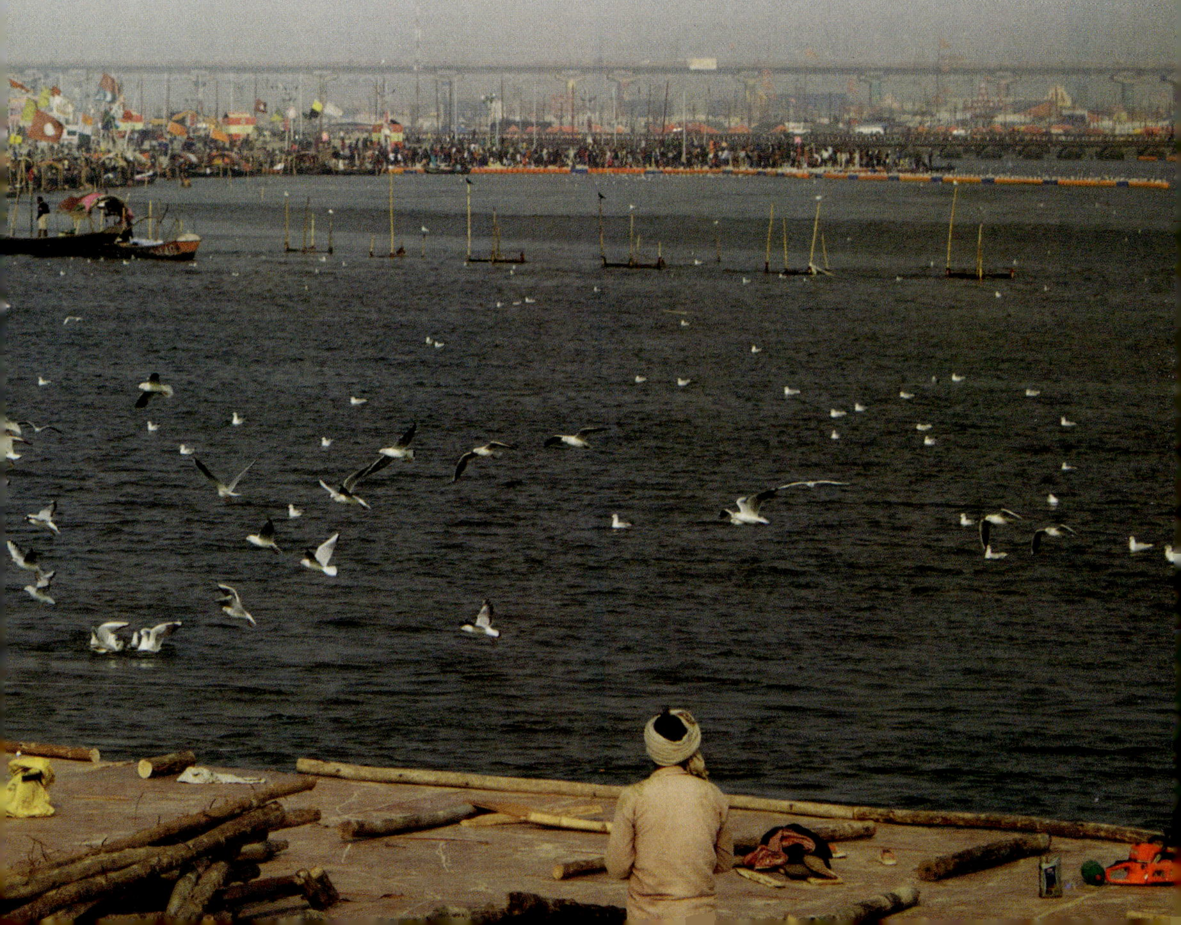

FOREWORD

The pictorial book *The Divine Kumbh* is a remarkable exploration of the Kumbh Mela, capturing its essence through stunning images and engaging text. The Kumbh Mela is a significant spiritual and cultural event in India, serving as a testament to the *dharma*, faith and spirituality that define the Indian ethos. It reflects our nation's rich cultural heritage.

I extend my blessings to the author, Deepak Sen, a resident of the sacred banks of the Ganga in Daraganj, Prayag, where the largest Kumbh Mela and Ardh Kumbh Mela take place. Deepak has truly felt the deep vibrations of the Kumbh Mela in his heart. This illustrated book covers all four Kumbh held at these holy sites.

The author and lensman has successfully captured various aspects of the Kumbh Mela through vivid images and thoughtful chapters. This book is not just a visual journey; it conveys the essence of this grand event. With ten engaging chapters, it explores the history of the Kumbh Mela and its significance in the 21st century.

Interestingly, while the world is now recognising the importance of rivers, our sages understood these thousands of years ago. The Kumbh is organised on the banks of the holy rivers confluence of Ganga, Yamuna and invisible Saraswati, Ganga, Shipra, and Godavari at Prayag, Haridwar, Ujjain, and Nashik, respectively. This highlights the significance of rivers and reminds us that every ancient civilisation developed along their banks, emphasising their vital role in our history.

Through this book, readers will gain valuable insights into the Kumbh Mela, deepening their understanding and appreciation of this magnificent celebration. It also fosters a greater awareness of our cultural traditions and illuminates the profound spirituality embodied in the Kumbh Mela.

स्वामी अवधेशानन्द ३ !

SHRI SWAMI AVDHESHANAND GIRI
Junapeethadhishwar Achary Mahamandleshwar

PREFACE

The word *Kumbh*, meaning 'pot', symbolically embodies a repository ranging from the darkest to the brightest aspects of life, encompassing both venom and nectar. As we embarked on documenting the Kumbh Mela, we were inundated with an infinity of information which inspired our camera shutters to capture diverse hues and moments, depicting movements and living murals. Each frame became a lexicon and a library of knowledge in itself. I cannot count the number of clicks that led to perfect pictures, nor can I fathom how many late nights were spent experimenting with the famous 'Monkey Theorem.' However, after completing this book, only one thought echoed in my mind, 'Dreams come true.'

While my humble thesis may lack the niceties of nuances, it is adorned with the tenderness of genuine history and statistically verified observations. It goes without saying that the Kumbh Mela is a significant Hindu pilgrimage and religious celebration. It is renowned as the world's largest peaceful gathering of people.

The Kumbh Mela takes place in four locations every twelve years.

PAGES 6–7: UNESCO's Intangible Cultural Heritage: Kumbh Mela

FACING PAGE: (ABOVE LEFT) Prayag Kumbh
(ABOVE RIGHT) Haridwar Kumbh,
(BELOW LEFT) Trayambak Simhastha Kumbh
(BELOW RIGHT) Ujjain Simhastha Kumbh

The Maha Kumbh Mela, considered the most important gathering in the Kumbh Mela cycle, sees millions of Hindu pilgrims congregating to bathe in holy rivers. This practice is believed to cleanse their sins and bestow spiritual merit. Elaborate ceremonies, religious discourses, processions of *sadhus* (Hindu holy men), and cultural performances enrich the occasion, showcasing the rich cultural and religious diversity of the participants.

The Kumbh Mela is not merely a site for repentance or remorse; it is also a vibrant platform for discourse. Majestic tents become homes for hermits, sages, and wise men during month-long stays, elevating Prayag to the status of the world's largest city by population. The mystical echoes of hymns, exhibitions of religious and mythological episodes, delectable delicacies, and more, contribute to making the Kumbh Mela an event that leaves indelible memories, offering experiences, excitement, and spiritual ecstasy.

My pen would be doing injustice if it failed to scribble heartfelt gratitude to Ravindra Kalia, the well-known Hindi author, Zafri Nofil, senior journalist, Press Trust of India and Prashant Kharote, Photographs. Special thanks to supporter like Sarvottamjee M. Jaipuriar & Dr Rajesh Tirpathi, who with their hawk-eyes, not only pinpointed the fallacies and follies in our creation, but also cemented it with their concrete suggestions for the betterment of book.

Deepak Kumar Sen

INTRODUCING KUMBH MELA

Kumbh Mela is one of the largest congregations of people on the earth. Millions, without any formal invitation, gather on the banks of four sacred rivers. They gather at the Sangam (the confluence of rivers Ganga, Yamuna and mythological Saraswati) in Prayagraj (erstwhile Allahabad), and on the banks of the Ganga at Haridwar, the Shipra at Ujjain and the Godavari at Nasik. They take ritual baths to purify and make themselves free from the vicious cycle of life and death, and move towards a heavenly realm, where suffering or pain does not exist.

In India, rivers are revered as goddesses and have their significance in the life of every Indian. Being an integral part of Indian culture and religion, no Hindu ritual is complete without their presence, physical or virtual. People prefer to perform the most important rituals of the Hindu religion on the banks of a river. An eternal life free of sins is the promise of the magnificent event of Kumbh.

Described as the 'greatest show on the earth', Kumbh is a symbol of integration, a vessel or pot, in which quintessential wisdom, spiritual thoughts, and human philosophy, as contemplated by saints and seers are accumulated. The values of age-old Indian culture, from which have emerged streams of human bliss, meet in a confluence to revive and awaken Indian society from its torpor.

Based on the movement of planets, the Purna (complete) Kumbh Mela is organised on the banks of a river once every twelve years, at four places—Prayag (Allahabad), Haridwar, Ujjain, and Nasik, in India. The Ardh (half) Kumbh Mela is held every six years at Haridwar and Allahabad (Prayag).

Maha Kumbh is held after 12 Purna Kumbh Melas, which is once every 144 years, at the confluence of rivers Ganga, Yamuna and mythological Saraswati. The Maha Kumbh Mela was organised at Prayag after 144 years in 2001.

Kumbh, dubbed as the world's biggest fair, is held at these places based on the specific zodiacal position of the Sun, the Moon, and the planet Jupiter. The venue for the next Kumbh Mela is chosen at the holiest time, occurring at the exact moment when these zodiacal conditions are fulfilled.

Astrologers calculate the exact date of the start of Kumbh after calculating the planetary motions with the help of Vedic astrology. The Sun moves in 12 zodiac signs in a year. Similarly, Jupiter also enters the zodiac once in 12 years. It is believed that during this period, drops of *amrit* (nectar) give mystical power to these places. Bathing at the river during Kumbh, at this moment, is believed to generate the greatest religious merit, but the Kumbh time is regarded as being so holy, that other bathing days are designated accordingly, weeks, or even months, before and after this climactic time.

Zodiacal positions of Jupiter, Sun and Moon

Place	River	Zodiac	Month
Haridwar	Ganga	Jupiter in Aquarius, Sun in Aries	Chaitra (March–April)
Prayag (Allahabad)	Ganga, Yamuna, & invisible Saraswati	Jupiter in Aries, Sun and Moon in Capricorn or Jupiter, and Taurus and Sun in Capricorn	Magh (January–February)
Trimbkeshwar, Nashik	Godavari	Jupiter in Leo or Jupiter, Sun and Moon in Cancer or Lunar Conjunction (Amavasya)	Bhadrapada (August–September)
Ujjain	Shipra	Jupiter in Leo, Sun in Aries or Jupiter, Sun and Moon in Libra on Kartik Amavasya	Vaishakha (April–May)

FACING PAGE ABOVE: Devotees experiencing a spiritual awakening at the Kumbh

FACING PAGE BELOW: Offering *tarpan* to gods and ancestors

It is to gain those powers that Kumbh has been celebrated in four places for as long as one can remember. Kumbh is held at an interval of 12 years in Haridwar, followed by melas in Prayag, Nasik and Ujjain, according to Indian astrology when:

पद्मिनी नायके मेषे कुम्भं राशिगतो गुरू: ।
गंगाद्वारे भवेद्योग: कुम्भ नाम ददोत्तमम् ।

Padminī nāyikā mēṣa
kumbha rāśi gata gurū:
Gaṅgā dvārē bhavēd yōga:
Kumbha nāma dadōttamam.

It means when Jupiter is in Aquarius and the Sun is in Aries during the Hindu month of Chaitra (March–April), the Kumbh happens to be at Haridwar.

माघेवृषगते जीवे मकरे चंद्र भास्करौ ।
अमावस्यां ततो योग: कुंभारव्यस्तीर्थ नायके ।

Māghē vṛṣa gatē jīvē makara
candra bhāskara.
Amāvasyā tō yōga: Kumbhāra
vyastīrtha nāyakē.

When Jupiter leaves the house of Aries and the Sun and Moon conjoin in Capricorn on the day of Amavasya during the Hindu month of Magha (January–February), the Kumbh Parva occurs in Prayag at the banks of the Ganges, Yamuna and mythological Saraswati.

मेष राशि गतो सूर्ये सिंह राशौ वृहस्पते ।
पूर्णिमायां भवेत कुम्भ:उज्जयिन्य: सुखप्रद ।

Mēṣa rāśi gatō sūrya sinha
rāśi vṛhaspati.
Pūrṇimāyāṁ bhavēta kumbha—
Ujjayin'ya—Sukhaprada.

It means when Jupiter is in Leo and Sun is in Aries, or when all three are in Libra during the Hindu month of Vaisakha (April–May), Kumbh happens in Ujjain on the bank of the river Shipra.

सिंहे गुरू यदा भानुश्चन्द्रश्चन्द्र त्रयस्तथा ।
गोदावर्या तदा कुम्भो जायतेअवनी मण्डले ।

Sinhē gurū yadā
bhānuścandraścandra trayastathā.

ABOVE: Tourists ride through the waters of the Sangam, surrounded by a stunning view of migratory birds, where nature and adventure meet

PAGES 16–17: Aerial view of the river bank at the confluence of holy rivers

Gōdāvaryāṁ tadā kumbhō
jāyatē'avanī maṇḍalē.

It means when the Sun and Jupiter are in Leo during the Hindu month of Bhadraprada (August–September), Kumbh occurs in Nasik on the bank of the Godavari.

Kumbh Mela has derived its name from the pot of nectar that gives immortality, as described in ancient Hindu scriptures such as the Puranas. *Kumbh* in Sanskrit language means pot or pitcher, and *Mela* means fair or festivity.

According to the myth of the Kumbh Mela—attributed to the

Puranas (collections of myth and legend) but not found in any of them—gods and demons fought over the pot (Kumbh) of nectar (Amrit), the elixir of immortality produced by churning the milky ocean.

During the struggle, drops of the elixir fell on the four places on the earth. The rivers there are believed to turn back into that primordial nectar at the climactic moment of each Kumbh Mela, giving pilgrims the chance to bathe in the essence of purity, auspiciousness, and immortality.

The name Kumbh has been derived from this mythic pot of elixir but is also the name for Aquarius, the sign of the Zodiac.

The origin of Kumbh, like any other tradition in India, is shrouded in a strange yet fascinating mix of myths, scientific reasoning, and historical and astrological theories. Three mythological stories are often

PAGES 20–21: A congregation of migratory birds graces the serene banks of the Sangam in Prayag in a harmonious blend of nature and spirituality.

LEFT: Close-up of a female devotee blowing a bejewelled conch

A sacred offering at the break of dawn

mentioned about the origin of Kumbh. One such popular tale includes Kashyap Rishi who had two wives, Diti and Aditi.

Diti gave birth to gods while Aditi gave birth to demons. They were in constant battle with each other, and once, the demons attacked the gods and defeated them. Led by Indra, the God of rain, the gods went to Brahma, the Creator, and narrated their ordeal.

Brahma then took them to Lord Vishnu, who suggested they collect various herbs and put them in the Kshirsagar (ocean of milk) and churn out nectar by using Mandara Mountain as a churning rod and the serpent king Vasuki as a *neti* (rope). And after drinking the nectar, gods would become immortal and strong.

The gods sought the help of demons for this sturdy task of Samudramanthan

A saint breaking into a grin while blessing devotees

and agreed to give them an share the elixir of immortality.

Lord Vishnu took the *avatar* (incarnation) of a turtle to support Mandara during Samudramanthan. For 1,000 years the ocean was churned with the demons holding Vasuki's head and the gods holding his tail.

During Samudramanthan, the first entity to appear was poison, which Lord Shiva drank. Due to this his throat became blue and he is called 'Neel Kanth' (the one with the blue throat). Apart from this, thirteen other opulent items, including the goddess of wealth Lakshmi, a gem Kaustubh, Parijat, Sura, the moon, Pushpak, the white elephant Airawat, a conch called Panchajanya, an apsara or beautiful dancing girl Rambha, a cow called Kamdhenu which could give unlimited quantities of milk, a white horse Uchaishrawa, and Dhanwantri, along with a pitcher (Kumbh) of the nectar of immortality, emerged.

As soon as the Kumbh emerged, Jayant, the son of Indra, took it away in the direction of gods, who did not want to share the nectar with demons. The gods thought that if it fell into the hands of demons then they would become strong and immortal. They would then rule the earth and evil would prevail.

Demons then chased Jayant and got him, but a battle ensued. The fight continued for 12 days and 12 nights. During this, Jayant kept the Kumbh at Prayag, Haridwar, Ujjain, and Nasik and it is said that a few drops of nectar were spilt at these places. As one day of the gods is equivalent to 12 years on the earth, therefore the festival is celebrated at the interval of 12 years, as during this period rivers become pure and give the power of *amrit* to worshippers.

RIGHT: Colours and emotions of the jostling crowd

PAGES 28–29: A beautiful panaroma of migratory birds the sacred Sangam at Prayag Kumbh

ABOVE: Adorned in marigold garlands and *rudraksh malas*, a *sadhu* sits meditating

FACING PAGE ABOVE: A sea of devotees at the river banks

FACING PAGE: Embracing tradition at Kumbh Mela, devotees enjoying the Shahi Snan

Then Lord Vishnu appeared as Vishwa Mohini to end the fight and lured the demons, and distributed *Amrit* among the gods. Jupiter, the Sun, Saturn, and the Moon were entrusted with the responsibility of preventing the nectar (elixir of immortality) from falling into the hands of the demons. The Moon was assigned to prevent nectar from spilling; the Sun to protect the pot from breaking; Jupiter to safeguard Jayant, and Saturn helped Indra.

As all these planets played a significant role, the Kumbh is held when these four are in a particular astrological position in the almanac. The other mythological stories often mentioned in the context of the the Kumbh include a popular tale about Durvasa Rishi. He once gave a necklace to rain god Indra, who in pride gave it to his elephant Airawat. The elephant threw it on the ground and trampled under his foot.

When Durvasa came to know about it, he cursed Indra, which led to suffering and hardship to all over the world. Then the gods and demons came together to churn the ocean. But as soon as nectar was found, demons took it away and kept it in Naglok.

Then Garuda, a bird on which Vishu flies, came to the rescue of the gods, and went to Naglok to bring the pitcher. On his way back, he placed the

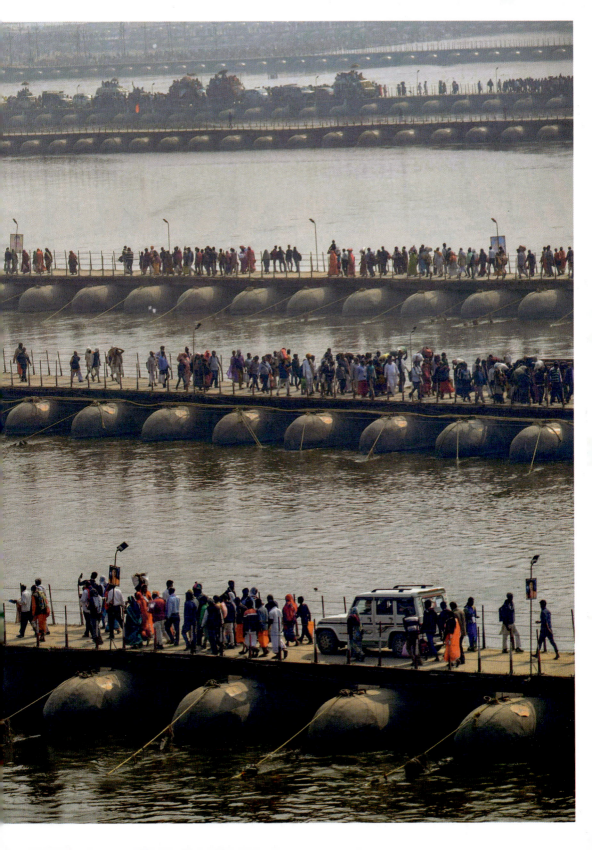

pot at the four places where the Kumbh is held now.

The third mythological narration about the origin of Kumbh is about Raja Prajapati Kashyap, who had two wives, Kadru and Vinta. They had an argument over the colour of the horses in the Sun god's chariot. They made a bet and the stakes were that the loser would serve as a slave to the other. Kadru took the help of her son, the serpent king, Naga Vasuki, and temporarily turned the colour of the horses from white to black.

Vinta, as a result, lost, and served as a slave to Kadru. But Kadru promised that she would release Vinta from slavery if Vinta could retrieve the pot of nectar from Naglok. Vinta's son Garuda took the task upon himself. When he succeeded in his endeavour, Indra tried to snatch the pitcher and a fight ensued. During this, nectar fell at four places, and Kumbh is celebrated at these places.

RIGHT: A congregation of devotees in a processsion to the Sangam

PAGES 32–33: Pontoon bridges at Prayag Kumbh, the largest spiritual gathering on the planet

HISTORY

The antiquity of Kumbh is still unclear, as there is no authentic written history. It is said, Megasthenes, a Greek ambassador to the court of King Chandragupta Maurya of Patliputra, visited the Kumbh Mela in the fourth century BC. Today, Patliputra is known as Patna, the capital of the eastern state of Bihar.

We get the first written evidence of the Kumbh Mela in the travelogue of Xuanzangor Hsuan Tsang, a Chinese-Buddhist monk, scholar, traveller, and translator, who travelled to India circa 630, during the reign of the famous Hindu king Harshvardhan.

In his eyewitness account, he wrote that half a million people had gathered on the banks of the Ganges at Prayagraj (Allahabad) during the Hindu month of Magha for Kumbh Mela. The King along with his ministers, scholars, philosophers, and sages, participated in the Mela celebrations, where he distributed gems and jewels, gold, silver, and even his clothes, in charity.

In the eighth century, when Hinduism was losing its relevance due to the advent and domination of Buddhism, Jainism and other faiths, a saint and religious reformer from southern India, Shankaracharya, popularised Kumbh as a religious gathering among the common masses.

FACING PAGE: A moment of serendipitous serenity between god's children

ABOVE: Pied Pier of Kumbh: A *sadhu* in ecstacy, leading the procession with his flute

FACING PAGE: A young devotee craddled by a *sadhu*

PAGE 38: A sadhu performs intricate yoga *asana*s

PAGE 39: Keeping the spiritual pulse of Kumbh Mela with ceremonial musical instruments

He successfully established the Kumbh Mela as a meeting place for people with religious and spiritual inclinations. As a natural consequence, with each passing year, more and more people started to attend the fair.

Later, Mark twain, the father of American poetry, wrote after visiting the Kumbh Mela in 1895:

'It is wonderful, the power of a faith like that, that can make multitudes upon multitudes of the old and weak and the young and frail enter without hesitation or complaint upon such incredible journeys and endure the resultant miseries without repining. It is done in love, or it is done in fear; I do not know which it is. No matter what the impulse is, the act born of it is beyond imagination, marvelous to our kind of people, the cold whites.'

We found a lot of literature about Kumbh in Sanskrit, Hindi, and other Indian languages. According to Sir Jadunath Sarkar, a noted historian and Bengali aristocrat:

'The first English account of the Kumbh that we have was written in 1796 when Haridwar was in the possession of the Marathas. On 8th April 1796, an English officer named Captain Thomas Hardwicke, accompanied by Dr Hunter paid a visit to Haridwar during the mela held on that date which was the Mesh Sankranti.'

In so many ways, the Kumbh Mela facilitates the coexistence of diverse traditions which have

RIGHT: A monk from an *akhara* performing as devotees watch in awe

partially sacrificed their theological, ideological, cultural, and social differences, in order to engage with one another and to seek understanding and even harmony.

Religious teachers from heterogeneous traditions, converge in this multi-cultural, multi-faith event with their own perspectives, purposes, and prejudices. While they share the same space with each other, many of them also share sentiments of mutual acceptance and assimilation and thereby impart the spirit of pluralism through their discourses at the Kumbh Mela.

LEFT: *Trishuls*, the weapon of Lord Shiva, are a common sight at the Mela

THE AKHARA

An *akhara* is basically an organised community or monastery of ascetic monks (*sadhus*) which maintains and follows its own tradition and practices. *Akhara* has come from the Sanskrit word *Akand* which means a place for practice (the Greek word 'Academy' has a similar meaning) for the protection of Sanatana dharma. Monastery or *Matt* is a religious order and *akharas* are their integral part. *Matts* are led by a head, known as Muttadheeshwar. These seers are well-versed in spiritual and religious scriptures and are also experts in using weapons.

FACING PAGE: A young saint strolling through the *akhara* grounds

An *akhara* is further divided into 8 *davas* (divisions) and 52 *marhis* (centers). Each *marhi* is governed by a Mahant. The top administrative body of an *akhara* is the Shree Panch, a body of five persons representing Brahma, Vishnu, Shiva, Shakti and Ganesh. It is elected at every Kumbh Mela, and members hold their post for a period of four years. Although, in Hinduism, people follow and offer prayers to a number of gods, most of them are either followers of Lord Shiva or Lord Vishnu. So, *akharas* are also divided into different types according to the following of the members.

Members of Shaiva Akharas are followers of Lord Shiva, Vaishnava

or Bairagi Akharas are followers of Lord Vishnu and the Kalpwasis are followers of Lord Brahma, the Creator. Udasins are followers of Sikhism. The history of *akharas* dates back to circa 2500 BCE, but they came into prominence during the 8th century CE when Adi Shankaracharya established seven *akharas* namely Mahaniravani, Niranjani, Juna, Atal, Avahan, Agni, and Anand, with an aim to strengthen the Hindu religion, and unite those practising different rituals, customs and beliefs.

The earliest recorded founding of an *akhara* was that of the Abhana in 547 CE. During Muslim rule in India and later in the times of British rule, they congregated and organised together, especially during the Kumbh Mela to work for the preservation of Hindu religion and culture. It is said that in 1565, Madhusudana Sarasvati started preparing *akharas* as an armed military force, to resist invasions by Muslims and protect Hindus. Shankaracharya divided the seers into two categories, Astradharis, of those who keep weapons, and Shaastradharis, those who are proficient in scripture.

The first group is generally known as Naga *sanyasis*, who are part of Dashnami Akhara. They are the followers of Shiva and Shakti and are the most violent. They are militant ascetics whose members formerly made their living as mercenary soldiers. They wield weapons to protect Hindu *dharma* from social evils. They could be easily identified by their naked, ash-smeared bodies. Their presence creates a great amount of curiosity among the Mela goers. Generally, they are the first to take a holy dip during Shahi Snans in the Kumbh Mela.

According to Sir Jadunath Sarkar, the first indisputable historical evidence of fighting Brahmans can be traced to Alexander's invasion of India

FACING PAGE ABOVE: Acharya Avdheshanand Giri of Juna Akhara at Shahi Snan

FACING PAGE BELOW: *Sadhus* of Juna Akhara proceeding for the royal bath

PAGES 48–49: Monks from the *akhara* entering the Kumbh Mela area

A large number of Naga *sadhus* on their way to the royal bath, carrying ceremonial flags

in 3 BCA. The Naga *sanyasi*s were called Gymnosophists by the Greeks, which means 'naked philosopher,' they are thus described by Arrian in his *Indica* in 2nd century CE. All other seers fall into the other category of Shaashtradharis. At present, there are three major *akhara*s: Dashnami or Naga, Bairagi and Nirmal. There are three minor *akhara*s: Atal affiliated with Mahanirvani, Anand affiliated with Niranjani, and Avahan affiliated with Juna. Furthermore, there is another small Brahmachari *akhara* named Agni which is also affiliated with Juna. Agni differs in a significant way as none of its members is a Naga *sadhu*. All Agni members claim to be *brahmin*s sworn to lifelong celibacy and refer to themselves as Brahmacharis.

*Sadhu*s sporting interesting tattoos entering the Kumbh Mela area

The biggest *akhara*s, going by the number of the saints, is Juna. Second is Niranjani, which is followed by Mahanirvani. The head of an *akhara* is called Acharya Mahamandaleshwar. Below him are in the hierarchy are other Mahamandaleshwaras, Mandaleshwaras and Shree Mahants. On the main bathing dates during the Kumbh Mela, the *akhara*s take out a colourful and magnificent procession of radiant saints sitting on chariots and elephants, which is witnessed by thousands of Kumbh visitors. The *sadhu*s, belonging to various *akhara*s take a dip in the holy river first, and only then are the ordinary pilgrims allowed to take a bath.

Dashnami or Naga (Nirvani) *sanyasi*s worship Lord Shiva, they

have the following seven *akhara*s: Mahanirvani, Atal, Niranjani, Anand, Juna or Bhairav, Avahan and and Panchagni.

Bairagis or Digamber are the worshippers of Lord Vishnu and they are mainly divided into three *akhara*s: Digamber, Nirvani and Shri Nirmohi Akhara. Followers or members of these *akahara*s wear clothes and have signs in particular colours, to differentiate themselves from others when they take out processions for Shahi Snan during the Kumbh or Ardha Kumbh. Nirmohis have a yellow-coloured sign, Digambers a motley-coloured one, and Nirvanis a silver-coloured sign. Bairagi *sadhu*s live in Kakh (ashes) and are members of these *akhara*s.

There is also the Udasin or Nirmal Akahara. The *sadhu*s following this sect call themselves Udasin. They have the following three *akhara*s: Panchayati Udaseen, Panchayati Akhara Naya Udaseen and Nirmal Panchayati Akhara. Besides these, there are *akhara*s of Kabirpanthi *sadhu*s also, which participate in the Kumbh and Ardh Kumbh.

Akharas and their Headquarters

Sampradaya	Name of Akhara's	Headquarters
Nirvani	Shri Panchayati Akhara Maharanirvani	Prayag (Allahabad)
	Shri Panch Atal Akhara	Varanasi
	Shri Panchayati Akhara Niranjani	Prayag (Allahabad)
	Topinidhi Shri Anand Akhara Panchayati	Nashik
	Shi Panchdashnam Juna Akhara	Varanasi
	Shri Panchdashnam Ahavan Akhara	Varanasi
	Shri Panchdashnam Panchagni Akhara	Junagarh
Bairagi Vaishnav Akharas	Shri Digambarani Akhara	Sabarkhantha
	Shri Nirvani Akhara	Ayodhya
	Shri Nirmohi Akhara	Mathura
Udasin	Shri Panchayati Baba Udasin	Prayag (Allahabad)
	Shri Panchayati Akhara Naya Udasin	Haridwar
	Shri Nirmal Panchayati Akhara	Haridwar

FACING PAGE: An *akhara* leader on his way to the royal bath

PAGES 54–55: An *akhara* precession carrying idols on caparisoned vehicles

Akharas are the heart and soul of the Kumbh Mela. The faith and respect that they command, bordering on veneration, is indescribable. Nirmohi Akhara was established in 1720 by Ramanandacharya. In 1885, it filed a lawsuit with the sub-judge of Faizabad in Uttar Pradesh to seek permission to build a temple to Lord Rama in Ram Chabutra, an area adjacent to the Babri Mosque.

The Juna Akhara, one of the largest, with about 400,000 ascetics, is divided into 52 lineages. It is fundamentally a Shaivite tradition established by Adi Shankaracharya, who is commonly held to be the first guru. Yet, the chosen deity of all 52 lineages is Guru Dattatreya, who is regarded as an avatar of Lord Vishnu. Hence, the ascetics of the Juna Akhara greet each other with 'Om Namo Narayana,' invoking one of the names of Vishnu, even though they worship Lord Shiva.

RIGHT: Procession of *babas* from the Shri Panch Dasnaam Aavahan Akhara

PAGES 58–59: A young Naga saint at Sangam bank blows on a ceremonial horn, ushering seekers.

The Juna Akhara tradition has not only embraced diverse Hindu deities and gurus, but has also accommodated Buddhists and Muslims within the tradition and exalted them as the head of their lineages. One of the 52 lineages of the Juna Akhara was established by Padmasambhava, also known as Guru Rinpoche, the 'Precious Guru.' Padmasambhava was instrumental in transmitting Vajrayana Buddhism to Tibet and is considered an avatar of Buddha Amitabha. Recognising that the Juna Akhara includes a lineage associated with the Vajrayana Buddhist tradition, the Dalai Lama often visits the Juna Akhara camp during Kumbh Melas.

In addition, there is another lineage known as the Multani Marhi of the Juna Akhara. It is called Multani Marhi because a Hindu-Sufi saint called Multani Baba, also known by Hindus as Keshav Puri Baba, and by Muslims

RIGHT: A foreign devotee receiving blessings from a Naga monk in the *akhara*

PAGES 62–63: Devotees and *sanyasi*s entranced in devotional wonder

Capturing the spiritual energy of the Kumbh

as Pir Shah Shams-i Tabriz, the teacher of Rumi, who established it. The tomb of Multani Baba is located just outside the city of Multan, Pakistan, with which his name is connected. Multani Baba had Hindu as well as Muslim disciples. He wrote books on both Sufi and Hindu subjects. When he left his body, he gave instructions that he be interred in a traditional Hindu *sanyasi* way, sitting in a meditative posture in an underground cave, with a *mala* in hand. He maintained, however, that a *qabr,* a Muslim grave, even if empty, should be built next to the *samadhi.*

Beyond the Juna Akhara, however, it is important to note that there are three Udasin *akhara*s, comprised

Naga *sadhu*s blessing devotees

of Sikhs following Guru Nanak and guided by *Guru Granth Sahib*, the Sikh scripture. These Udasin ascetics are also an integral part of the traditional *akharas* present at the Kumbh Mela.

Diksha, or initiation into the *akhara* orders takes place at the Kumbh Mela. It is hard to tell, when their bodies are adorned with ashes, whether these are the ashes of another life, or the ashes of the fire that they keep burning in their tent compounds. They are conquerors of death.

At the Kumbh Mela, some of the more flamboyant *sadhu*s enact their indifference to discomfort and pain by holding one arm in the air for years, lying on a bed of nails, or

ABOVE: Devotees carrying divine idols into the Kumbh Mela area

PAGES 68–69: An *akhara* leader accompanied by his entourage

sitting in meditation in an iron swing hung over a burning fire. Typically, they go barefoot winter and summer, conquering cold and heat. Their flagrant rejection of the comforts of settled life empowers them in a world dominated by consumerism and the concept of what they call 'getting and keeping.'

Historically, the basic purpose of setting up *akhara*s was to form a band of religious warriors (*dharma sainik*s) who would protect and safeguard *dharma* from social evils. During the Kumbh Mela, the ceremonial procession of the *akhara*s and the Naga *sadhu*s has all the trappings of royalty and is believed to be an auspicious sight. The Mahant is seated on a silver throne placed upon a caparisoned elephant. Around him, hundreds of Naga *sadhu*s, with their ash-smeared bodies and lances, march on foot.

Camels and horses, which are also part of the procession, signify the old Hindu concept of the four-limbed army or *Chaturanga Sena*. They move towards the holy waters of the Ganges for the ritual dip. However, Mahanirvani Akhara is the most important of all and it is normally the first to take the Shahi Snan. Their *peshwai* (entry) and subsequent bath in the holy Ganga, officially marks the beginning of the Maha Kumbh.

*Akhara*s of Nagas still monopolise the holiest spots at each Kumbh Mela, during the most propitious moments, and although the government now enforces an established bathing order, history records bloody disputes between groups vying for precedence. Shorn of all clothing, having renounced all material aspects of worldly life (at least in theory) with their pledge of *sanyas*, and with their bodies smeared with *vibhuti* (holy ash), Naga *sadhu*s have a reputation for being volatile and unpredictable in their behaviour. This also helps keeping others at a distance.

THE NAGA

In Kumbh, Naga *sadhu*s (ascetics) or the Nagas are the most photographed but least understood cult members. They mostly remain aloof from the civilisation, and very rarely appear in public. Kumbh Mela is said to be one of those rare events where the common population get a chance to see them. During this, they could be seen at the Mela area adorned with jewellery, trinkets, *trishul, damru,* and *rudraksha malas*.

The picture of thousands of ash-smeared Naga *sadhu*s wearing nothing but marigold garlands, shrieking in ecstacy and marching under the huge flags, signs, and banners of assorted *akhara*s of Dashnami ascetics, on their way to the Shahi Snan at the confluence of the Ganga, Yamuna, and mythical Saraswati is the most important feature of the Kumbh Mela, and no photograph is complete without this. It also presents India's spiritual image to the world.

The procession of Naga *sadhu*s attracts a large number of visitors to the Mela, due to the various myths associated with them. Tourists from every corner of the world flock to the Kumbh to watch Naga *baba*s mediating and performing various rituals, in their out–of–the–world appearance.

FACING PAGE ABOVE: A *sadhu* pulls at a *chillum* at night

FACING PAGE BELOW: A sadhu lost in transcendent ecstasy

ABOVE: Amid the swirling smoke, a *sadhu*'s pursuit to free himself from earthly elements
PAGES 74–75: Captivating sight of the keepers of ancient wisdom

Naga *sadhu*s basically belong to a group of ascetics who have renounced the materialistic world and practised celibacy to escape from the cycle of birth and death to attain *moksha*. The unique characteristic features of these saints include the fact that they remain naked, even in biting cold. They smear their bodies with a layer of ash, wear heavy coils of matted hair on their head, hold tridents or any weapon, and smoke marijuana through a pipe called *chillum* or 'Shiv Muli'. They draw their inspiration for living such a life from Lord Shiva. But there is also another aspect of these Shaivite

Young Shaiv *sadhu*s bearing *trishul*s with pride and devotion embody the fierce spirit of Lord Shiva at Kumbh Mela.

saints. They are militant in nature and always ready to fight for Hinduism as religious warriors.

Historically, the Naga tradition began in the 8th century when a Hindu seer and exponent of Advait philosophy, Adi Shankaracharya created them as a Hindu army to protect Sanatan Dharma, and Hinduism in extension. Born in Kalady, in Kerala, Shankaracharya left home at the age of five to travel across India. He created the Dashnaam Sanyas ashrams primarily with members from the Giris (mountain sects), Puris (dwellers of towns and cities), Saraswatis (priests),

Van-Aranyaks (forest hermits), and Sagar (seaside sects).

Realising the need for *shaastra* (knowledge) as well as *shastra* (weapons), Adi Shankaracharya preserved *shaastra* for the Acharyas and made *shastra* the ornament of the Nagas. Nagas are part of Dashnami ascetics (*akhara*s), who are militant Shaivites. They can belong to any of the 10 religious orders (Dashnam means 'ten names') founded by Adi Shankaracharya.

All Dashnami Akharas have ascetics of any or all 10 orders, and they have names that reflect this allegiance: Aranya, Ashram, Bharti, Giri, Parvata, Puri, Saraswati, Sagara, Tirtha and Vana. With their deep veneration for Adi Shankaracharya, they still chant, 'Shankaram Shankaracharya Keshavam Badyarayanan, Sutra-bhashyakatobande Bhagwatepunah-punah', which means 'I am that Shiva,

RIGHT: A timeless connection to the divine is felt in the presence of the Naga *sadhu*s.

PAGES 78–79: The *sadhu*s of Kumbh, living embodiments of renunciation, walking the path of spiritual freedom and devotion

The colours of devotion, painted in the light of spirituality

born in every age to save the world from itself.' This is the Shaivite equivalent of the famous sayings of Lord Krishna in Bhagwad Gita, 'Dharma Samsthapanaarthya Sambhavaami Yugeyuge'. It is said that it was these militant Nagas who were instrumental in winning back Hinduism from Buddhism. They even laid their lives to protect Hinduism during an attack in 1757 by the Afghan invader Ahmed Shah Abdali on Gokul and Vrindavan, the fabled birthplace and playground of Lord Krishna. The Afghan invader sent hordes of his soldiers into the holy places, to loot, plunder, and rape.

He had to face stiff resistance from the Hindu Jat prince Jawahar

Joy in every heart, faith in every step

Singh, who ruled the Barj-Matsya region. The holy city of Mathura was ransacked and brutalised by Abdali's soldiers after the death of the Jat prince's 10,000 soldiers. Temples were destroyed and at many holy places, women jumped into Yamuna to save themselves from rape. The Afghan had given orders to, '[m]ove into the boundaries of the accursed Jat, and in every town and district held by him, slay and plunder. The city of Mathura is a holy place of the Hindus...let it be put entirely to the edge of the sword. Up to Agra leave not a single place standing.'

Vrindavan, which is about 11 km north of Mathura, could not

escape this fate. Much wealth was displayed in its many temples. Here Abdali's general Jahan Khan and Najib plundered the town with 20,000 men, and another general massacre was carried out against the inoffensive monks of the most pacifist order of Vishnu worshippers, (c. 6 March 1757).

One of the diary entries of the Afghan ruler's diarist records a visit to Vrindavan:

> Wherever you gazed you beheld heaps of slain; you could only pick your way with difficulty, owing to the number of bodies lying about and the amount of blood spilt. At one place that we reached, we saw about 200 dead children lying in a heap. Not one of the dead bodies had a head... The stench and effluvium in the air were such that it was painful to open your mouth or even to draw breath.

LEFT: *Sadhus*, the spiritual guardians of timeless wisdom

ABOVE: Purifying the soul in the holy waters

PAGES 86–87: A centuries-old tradition, alive in every ritual

After Vrindavan, it was the turn of Gokul, Lord Krishna's birthplace. Sardar Khan, prime general of the Afghans, launched an attack on Gokul, but here, thousands of ash-smeared warrior monks stopped them. The Naga *sadhu*s armed with swords, matchlocks, and cannons, had gathered after calling together their wandering bands, to rise in defence of *dharma*.

Stirred by the atrocities of the Afghans and Muslim rulers, bands of Naga *sadhu*s and assorted holy men, coalesced into larger groups, often numbering more than 10,000, to provide protection to the temples, to travel routes, and even to towns and rival armies.

For many centuries these Naga monks and their disciples began to

Offering prayers, seeking peace, forging connections

take up arms amid the upheavals in northern India. During the fall of the Mughal Empire, they emerged as a serious force to reckon with.

Their notable leader Rajendra Giri Gosain, from whose time we have a correct and written history of the Nagas, held such a reputation of bravery that his band of Nagas would contend with enemies who outnumbered them more than ten times over, with utter abandon and fury.

Later on, some of the larger bands, under Himmat Bahadur and Anupgir Gosain, lead vast armies across the northern Indian plains. The notorious Afghan cavalry launched itself against the Nagas just to face a wild and reckless counter charge. The Nagas, displaying utter disregard for their own lives, forced the Afghan attackers to retreat in confusion and defeat.

After some time the Afghans, with reinforcement, returned to the attack. and a bitter struggle ensued. The Afghans were fighting for loot, plunder and rape, while the Naga *sadhu*s, who had already given up their worldly and material attachments, and were participants in a long tradition of warfare, fought solely for *dharma* and faith.

The battle cry of the Nagas, 'Har Har Mahadev' and of the Afghans, 'Ya Ali' rose above the groans and shrieks of the wounded and dying. The battle continued even as dusk fell and they fought while stepping on the bodies of the slain, but still, the Nagas did not give ground. Enraged, Abdali then sent more troops into the battle. The yet undefeated soldiers of Abdali, who had marched victoriously from the borders of India to Central Asia, were met with renewed charges and attacks from the Naga *sanyasi*s. They

RIGHT: Initiation ceremony of a female *sadhvi* at the Sangam

fought so fiercely that the Afghans began to lose hope of victory. Their leader Sardar Khan called a retreat after the Afghan army suffered huge losses, and the Afghans fell back in defeat and humiliation. The holy town of Gokul was saved but at an appalling cost of human life.

The Naga *sadhus* not only saved the shrines and the thousands of refugees inside them, but they exemplified the age-old tradition of valour mixed with *dharma*—the concept of rising in arms each time they were called upon. They went on to fight bitter, decade-long struggles with the British in India. This history was famously celebrated in the late 19th-century novel *Ananda Math*. Their exploits became the inspiration for the freedom fighters of the 20th century. Keeping up with their military traditions, they call their retreats Chhavni or army camps, to this day. They hold mock jousts using words, spears and tridents, during the Kumbh Mela.

Being a militant sect, it is said that it isn't unusual for them to strike to kill someone on issues of honour, even during a Kumbh Mela. Noted historian Sir Jadunath Sarkar, in his book on Dashnami Akharas, wrote:

The first indisputably historical evidence that we find of fighting Brahmans occurs in the course of Alexander's invasion of India in 3 BC when after crossing the river Ravi in pursuit of Malaya people... The Naga Sannyasis were called by the Greeks "Gymnosophists," which literally means "naked philosopher", they are thus described by ancient Greek writer Arrian in his book.

The philosophers (Brahmans) from the caste most esteemed in reputation and dignity, no necessity is incumbent upon them to any bodily labour... nor have they any compulsory duty except to offer sacrifice to the gods on

FACING PAGE ABOVE: Initiation ceremony of a Naga *sadhu* on the banks of the Ganga at Prayag
FACING PAGE BELOW: After *diksha*, the Nagas become symbols of strength and spirituality.

behalf of the commonwealth of India. These philosophers pass their lives naked in the winter, in the sun under the open sky, but in the summer when the sun holds sway, they live in the meadows and in the marshes under the great trees…

Why Nagas live naked is a question which arouses curiosity among the common population. They, in their cryptic words, will say that this is in order to 'become detached to attain salvation in order to set themselves free from the vicious cycle of birth and death'.

For complete detachment, you have to shed your clothes. They have logic to this. Even if you have just clothes on your body, you would need to clean them to wear them. While washing them, you need another set of clothes. After washing, you need to keep them at some place to wear them the next time, for that you would need a bag. If you have a bag then you will have to take care of it, so that you don't lose it or have it stolen from you. This in fact leads to attachment. So the Nagas, to save themselves from these unwanted attachments, decide to remain naked. Naga *sadhus* are supposed to be so deeply spiritual and devoted to god, that they don't care about how they look, and also about the weather, if it is warm or cold.

Describing the differences between Nagas and other *sadhus*, Sir Sarkar has written:

The sannyasis worship Shiva in the ordinary way and Shakti (or Shiva's female consort) with a special secret ritual called marga of salvation. As Shiva himself wears a rosary of Rudraksha seeds, every sannyasi does the same. A rudraksha seed with only one line of depressions (Ek Mukhi) is considered to have the greatest sanctity and mystic power… The Nagas and Tapaswis smear their whole body with ashes (regarded as the Bibhuti of Shiva the Yogi), other Sannyasis only mark Tripundarik (three lines) with ashes on their forehead, and similar lines on eleven other places of the body, the whole being known as Dwadash Bibhuti.

To become a Naga, any male has to go through a 'must-follow' set of esoteric initiation rituals, according to the secret Dashami rules. One has to spend several years devoted to his Guru, and pass four important stages. First, an aspirant becomes a *chela* or a *brahmachari* (disciple) in an *akhara*. He has to serve his Guru with total devotion.

After serving in the Akhara to his Guru's satisfaction, he then progresses to become Mahapurush, later, an Avdhoot, and finally a Naga. The last of these rituals to become a Naga, held after midnight, is notable for the mark it leaves on the man. At the appointed time, an aspirant who wants to join the Akhara stands next to a *kirtistambh* (triumphal column), accompanied by four Shri Mahants and an Acharya Guru who assigns him a *mantra*. A Mahant then pulls the foreskin of his penis back thrice, forcefully, snapping the membrane underneath, which restrains it. It is called the *tang tode* ceremony. Only after this ritual does a *sanyasi* qualify fully as a Naga and over time, prolonged exposure desensitises the penis to an extent.

The *tang tode* may be performed in symbolic or token ways as well, but the Naga, often seen with smoking marijuana in a *chillum*, decorated with ashes, and dancing on vedic chants is the most important attraction of the Mela. The consumption of *bhang* or opium is also considered to be a part of the ritual performed by Naga *sadhu*s. It is said in the holy scriptures that doing so will lead them to eternity or *nirvana*. The authenticity of Naga-hood is determined by the status of the ascetic's sexual organ. The Nagas are forbidding and would not do anything that would help in demystifying them. 'Don't mess with us' would be an apt refrain for them.

MOKSHA AND KUMBH

The concept of *moksha* has been debated and dissected by every generation since time immemorial. Many schools of thought have interpreted and defined *moksha* in the garb of specific genres and nuances. For me, *moksha* is a symbol of an individual's conscious state of spiritualism. Indian philosophy opens the door and relieves us from the cycle of birth and rebirth. This is called *moksha* or salvation.

The way to attain *moksha* has been a point of consistent and concerted contemplation among the sagacious sapiens of the Hindu society. Amid an array of other measures, the Kumbh- a

mythical but auspicious and sacred pot, filled with nectar, is believed to pave the way for the trans-state of *moksha*. *Moksha* is an integral component of four goals including *purushartha* or the value of *arth* (money), *kama* (fulfilment of desires), and *dharma* (duty), prescribed for the practitioners of Sanatan Dharma. Kumbh is one of the main parts of the Indian philosophy of salvation or *moksha*, which is of highest value in the Hindu religion. The soul receiving *moksha* is compared to a drop of water merging into the vast ocean which represents the Supreme Soul (God).

The Shahi Snan or 'royal bath' at Kumbh and Ardh Kumbh are both related to *moksha*. All the pilgrimages

FACING PAGE: Kumbh Mela, where earth meets the heavens in devotion

gather at the bank of holy rivers, as they think a holy dip during Shahi Snan is one of the ways to *moksha*. One of the myths about Prayag Kumbh substatiates this. In earlier times, a few devotees jumped into Sangam from the fort of Prayag (Allahabad), which is close to the river, from their own wish to sacrifice their life, because they believed this was the best way for *moksha*.

> If one bathes and sips water where the Ganga, Yamuna, and Sarasvati meet, he enjoys liberation, and of this there is no doubt.
>
> —*Padma Purana*
> *Uttara Khanda* (23.14)

> Those who bath in the bright waters of the Ganga where they meet the dark waters of the Yamuna during the month of Magh will not be reborn, even in thousands of years.
>
> —*Matsya Purana* (107.7)

LEFT: At Kumbh Mela, the quest for Moksha unfolds in the sacred waters, guided by the presence of Naga *sadhu*s.

ABOVE: A Hindu saint practicing yoga *asana*s in the spirit of spirituality after a sacred bath

PAGES 100–101: Dramatic Naga *sadhu*s before the holy dip, embodying their strength and devotion

In this section, we will venture to unveil a general introduction to the term *moksha*, which according to Hinduism, is bestowed by God who is the giver of *moksha* to the worshipper, if the worshipper completely surrenders himself. The other idea is that humans by their own efforts and good *karma* can attain *moksha*.

The important point of agreement among the various schools of Indian philosophy is the recognition of liberation or release (Moksha) from the cycle of rebirths, as the highest of

Hindu saint performing rigorous yoga *asana*s after the sacred bath

human ends or values. The Indians generally speak of four values—*artha, kama, dharma* and *moksha*. Of these, the first two, which respectively mean 'wealth' and 'pleasure', are secular or purely worldly values. The other two, whose general meaning has already been indicated, may, in contrast, be described as spiritual.

If *karma* is the cause of births and rebirths, pain, and pleasure, then *moksha* is the supreme goal of worshippers in all religions. Release from birth and rebirth, or knowing

ABOVE: Harmony, devotion and celebration under one sky

FACING PAGE: Celebrating unity in diversity through faith and tradition

your own true self. This is why I have defined *moksha* as the greatest good. Different schools of Indian philosophy have different rules for the attainment of *moksha*.

Moksha in the Vedas

In Vedas, it is clearly iterated that the *atman* and *brahman* are two synonyms terms. If we see four *mahavakya*s (important quotes) of the Vedas, they are 'Ahm bramhasmi', 'Ayamatma Brahman', 'Tattvamasi', and 'Pragyanam Bramhan'. They all indicate that knowing the pure form of *atman* as *brahman* is the chief aim of human life.

The diversity of everyday experience may only be an appearance of *brahman* and therefore false, as one school of interpreters of the Upanishads holds, but, even according

to the other school, it is not the whole of truth, for unity also is equally real.

Yet diversity appears to be the sole truth, owing to an inveterate habit of our mind which can be traced to our *avidya* (ignorance) of the ultimate reality. This is what is meant by *maya*—the power or the principle that conceals from us the true character of reality.

When Maya functions it hides Bramhan and it presents what is not real. If ignorance is the cause of birth and rebirth, then *jnan* (*gyan* or knowledge) is the only way to obtain *moksha*. Ignorance may be regarded as negative, that is, as merely a lack of knowledge of the unity underlying the diversity given in common experience; or it may be looked upon as positive in the sense that it gives rise to misapprehensions, making us see the manifold world, where there is *brahman* and only *brahman*.

Moksha in Upanishads

Delving deep into the issue, we find there is not much difference between

LEFT: At Kumbh Mela, the path to *moksha* is illuminated by devotional surrender.

what the Veda advocates and what the Upanishad promulgates about *moksha*. However, we have already maintained that the Upanishads are different from the Vedas. The Vedas consist of two parts, *Poorvamimansa* (*Karmkand*) and *Uttarmimansa* (*Jnankand*).

Vedas are more concerned about *karma* whereas Upanishads are about *jnan* (knowledge).

In Upanishadic teaching, knowing the true nature of self or *atman* as *bramhan* is *moksha*. It is clearly mentioned in the Upanishads that knowing ourselves as *brahman* is the only way to liberation.

It is clearly mentioned in the Upanishads that knowing ourselves as *brahman* is the only way of liberation. *Moksha* in Upanishads is freedom from bondage. *Avidya* is bondage, *vidya* is *moksha*. Vidya is knowledge of *brahman* and *atman* as one, and manifest in all creatures. *Moksha* is becoming Brahma (*bramha bhavna*) becoming all (*sarva bhavna*), the vision of the self of the universe (*ek atmadarsana*). It is complete autonomy (*svarajya*) or freedom (*ananda*).

Moksha in the Geeta

The holy *Bhagvat Geeta* suggests three ways to achieve *moksha*. These are Karma yoga, Bhakti yoga, and Jnan yoga. The supreme experience is freedom, and the *Jnan* refers to both the goal of the adventure as well as the path leading to it.

According to some thinkers, *jnan* is a superior path, as compared to the other methods of approach, and that cognition alone persists, while the other emotions will fall away in the supreme state of freedom. There does not seem to be any justification for such an opinion. Freedom or *moksha* is unity with the Supreme Self. It is called by different names: *mukti* or release; *brahmi sthiti* or being in *brahman*; *naiskarmya* or non-action; *nistraigunya* or the absence of the three qualities; *kaivalya* or solitary salvation; *brahmanbhava* or the being of *brahman*.

FACING PAGE: Detailed close-up of a *sadhu*'s adornments of sacred beads and silver charms

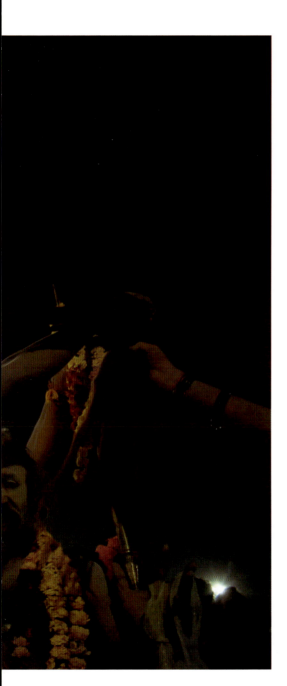

In the absolute experience, there is the feeling of the oneness of all. A freed soul is beyond all good and evil. Virtue is transcended in perfection. The *mukta* rises above any mere ethical rule of living, to the light, largeness, and power of spiritual life. Even if he should have committed any deeds which would in ordinary circumstances necessitate another birth on the earth, no such thing is necessary. He is freed from ordinary rules and regulations.

Moksha in Sankhya

When we study Sankhya philosophy, we don't find the concept of *moksha*, as stated in other schools of Indian philosophy. According to Sankhya, *moksha* is *viveka* (discrimination) of the *purusha* (self) from the *prakriti* (non-self) and its modification. It is knowledge due to *viveka* (discrimination), of the difference between *purush* and *prakriti*. It cannot be known by *karmakand* (action) because *karma* is possible only

LEFT: *Sadhus* performing a ceremonial dance under the night sky

with *gunas* (subtle entities or qualities) and *moksha* is *nistregunya* (free from all qualities). When *purush* realises its own from to be entirely different from *achetan* (lifeless), *prakriti* and *antahkaran* (man-mind), *buddhi* (intellect) and *ahankar* (ego). It is *vivek jnan* (discrimination).

Moksha in Yog Philosophy

Patanjali says in his *Yogsutra*,

पुरूषार्थशून्यानांगुणानांप्रतिप्रसव: कैवल्यंस्वरूपप्र तिष्ठावाचितिशक्तेरिति ।

Here it is said that cessation of *avidya* is *moksha* or *kevalya*. By the *purusharth* (efforts) of man, qualities (*sattva rajas* and *tamas*) becomes nil, which means, they go from whence they came (*pratiprasav*). *Chitishakti* (*atman*) which knows and enjoys its own form is *kaivalya*. According to Patanjali, after attaining *kaivalya*, man has no rebirth, just as baked seeds cannot sprout after they are baked.

Yoga is regarded as a branch of Sankhya, as all the doctrines of the Sankhya on cosmology, physiology, and psychology have been simply adopted by Yoga. So too, the doctrine of emancipation is the same. Along with the theory of the conception of the soul from matter, the theory that this emancipation is effected solely by means of a clear distinction drawn between matter and spirit, is also taken from Sankhya.

Patanjali has defined Yoga as the cessation of the modification of *chitta*. *Chitta* signifies the three internal organs of Sankhya—*buddhi* or intellect, *ahankar* or ego, and *manas* or mind:

Modification of chitta are of five kinds (1) Right cognition (Pramana) (2) Wrong cognition (Viparyaya), (3) Verbal cognition or Imagination (Vikalpa) (4) Absence of cognition or sleep (Nidra) and (5) Memory (Smriti).

FACING PAGE: Where the sacred waters offer the promise of *moksha*

PAGES 112–113: A procession of *akhara* leaders accompanied by their entourage and devotees

Patanjali suggests his Ashtang Yoga (eightfold path) for *moksha*. From Ashtang Yoga one gets *moksha*.

Moksha in *Nyaya*

Upvarg or *moksha* is the absolute cessation of pain and rebirth. The *Nyay Sutra* claims that the bondage of the world is due to false knowledge, which can be removed by constantly thinking of its *pratipakshabhavna* (opposite). True knowledge destroys false knowledge which generates attachment, aversion, and delusion, which are the springs of action. When the cause of *dukkha* (sorrows), *jnama* (birth), private actions for the fulfilment of desires, *dosh* (faults), and *mithya jnan* (false knowledge) sequentially vanish, then the root cause of these things is eliminated, and then one obtains *upvarg*.

According to Vatsayayan, who is a commentator on the *Nyay Sutra*, 'The fruition of all one's action comes about

RIGHT: Experiencing the divine energy of Kumbh Mela in the pilgrimage of a lifetime

Embracing the essence of Moksha amid the vibrant tapestry of Kumbh

in the last birth preceding release.' Nyay philosophy does not accept *anand* (joy) in the state of liberation, it says liberation is release from pain. Dr Radhakrishan comments on the Nyaya view of *moksha*, 'It is defined negatively as the cessation of pain and not as the enjoyment of positive pleasure for pleasure is always tainted with pain.'

Moksha in Advait Vedant

Shankar has given us a theory of the concept of *maya* (illusion) or *adhyas* (superimposition). According to Advait Vedant philosophy, this world is

Evening *aarti* performed by a priest

adhyas of Brahma. It is only an illusion that the world is real and changeless.

It is because of *maya* or *avidya* (false knowledge), that *jiva* falls into bondage. Pure soul or *atman* is mixed with beginning-less *avidya*, like milk with water, in such a way that the natures of both do not appear separate.

The mind is *maya*'s product but *jiva* believes that these are his attributes. It does not separate itself from it, and does not feel its true form.

According to Shankar, there are three signs of *moksha* in every man freed from his body. There are three types of bodies i.e. *sthool, suksham,* and *karan*. *Avidya* vanishes with *vidya* or *jnan*. In *moksha* one has realisation of self as *brahman*. It is possible only with *jnan*.

Moksha in Vishishtadvait

Ramanuja insists that the *karmas* should be performed in an absolutely disinterested manner, simply to please god. When the soul performs these actions, it will realise that only this performance cannot lead to liberation. According to Ramanuja, bondage of the *jiva* is due to *avidya*, *karma*, *vasna* (desires) and *ruchi* (affection).

> For obtaining release from samsara, the soul has to remove the karmic obstacles, it has to purify itself from the dross and dust of karma that have somehow surrounded it. This can be done by a harmonious combination of action and knowledge.

RIGHT: *Devotees thronging to the river bank at Sangam*

Jnan is identified by Ramanuja as the highest *bhakti* or devotion which is obtained by *prapatti* (self-surrender) and by a constant *dhruva smriti* (remembrance of god as the only object of devotion). In Ramanuja's philosophy, obtaining the qualities of god and realising the true form of god is *moksha*.

According to Advaita, to remain as the Self is release, *moksha* is the Self. To attain the Self is to attain *moksha*.

Other Indian religions like Jainism, Buddhism and Sikhism have a deep belief in *moksha*.

Buddhism has suggested the eight fold path for cessation of suffering. Dr Radhakrishnan says that according to Buddhism,

The horizon of being is extended to the limits of reality. It is kinds of existence devoid of egoism, a timeless existence, full of confidence, peace, calm, bliss, happiness, delicacy, parity, freshness.

In Jainism *sanvar* and *niriara* are two kinds of *kaivalya* or *moksha*.

Madhavacharya explains in his book,

Some people collects good karma (Punya) in their inner feelings (sanvar) and some destroy bad karmas (Pap) nirjara. The person who gets four things jnan, darshan, Veerya and sukkha is not bound, and the soul whose eight karmas are destroyed gets infallible liberation.

FACING PAGE ABOVE: The Mela offers an interesting backdrop to all kinds of seekers

FACING PAGE BELOW: *Akhara* performers

PAGES 122–123: Naga *sadhus* leading the way to the Shahi Snan

Sect-Marks or Tilak

Marks or Tilak of the Shaiv Sect

Shaiv Sect

Shaivite Sect

Marks or Tilak of the Vaishnava Sect

Ramanandi

Madhavacharya

Nimbarka

Vallabhacharya

Ramanujis of Southern India

Bargal

Tingal

Sakta Sect

Red dot

THE TILAK

Tilak ('mark' in English) is a paste made of ash, sandalwood, vermillion, clay, or turmeric, typically worn on the forehead, and sometimes other parts of the body like the torso, arms, or neck, signifying which spiritual lineage a devotee adheres to, within Hinduism. The shape of the *tilak* and the substance it is made from generally corresponds to the god or goddess that lineage worships.

The *tilak* on the saints' forehead is necessary as it allows people to identify his *sampradaya* (sect). These *tilak* on the foreheads of saints from different Akharas, communities, and sects, are also an attraction for the pilgrims.

The *sadhu*s and worshipers have different beliefs regarding the marking on their bodies. There are three communities which use sandalwood, *gopi chandan*, and *roli* as *tilak*. The saints from the Vaishnav sect wear *udharvpund*, Shaiv sect wear *tripund*, and Shakti sect wears *roli*.

According to Mahant Nritya Gopal Das, the *tilak* and the hair exhibit Hindu culture and these are ornaments for men. Brahamachari Bapoli of the Vaishanav sect says *tilak* helps the *sadhu*s to rise above conscious, dreamy, and semi-conscious stages. It becomes a means to attain god.

FACING PAGE: Primary order of *tilak*s or sect marks

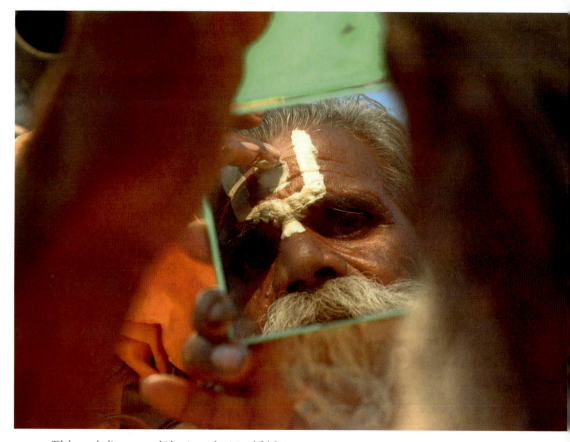

*Tilak*s symbolise personal identity and spiritual fidelity

About the physical importance of *tilak*, he said that in the present scenario, man indulges in worthless thoughts. A kind of energy emerges on his forehead and the *tilak* enables the *sadhu*s to control it.

*Sadhu*s of Shaivite and Vaishnavite sects claim that *tripund* and *udharpund* represent their gods— Lord Shiv and Lord Vishnu.

The colours used in the *tilak* also have their own importance, like— red or saffron is used in the *tilak* to symbolise *shreevatsa* or Lord Vishnu's *chakra*. Ashes are used in Shiva's *tilak*. Among some caste groups, *gorochan*, saffron, or blue-coloured *tilak* is also applied. In short, applying *tilak* in Hinduism is a symbol of the authority of god, which makes a person feel spiritual and closer to god.

The followers of the Shakti sect wear *roli* or black *tilak*. They call it a shining point. Delhi's Kapalik Mahakaal Bhairav Nath Saraswati said that according to the Hindu culture, for a woman, her *suhag* is of foremost importance. She wears a red *roli*. It is smeared in a straight line to show that the wearer would not be unlucky. It shows that god is one.

Apart from this, applying *tilak* also means that the person believes in the deities of Sanatan Dharma and their grace. Secondly, *tilak* is considered a way for the person to get the power and blessings of the god. That's why applying *tilak* on the forehead is an important ritual in Hinduism. It is considered important both religiously and socially.

Applying *tilak* is considered auspicious in Hinduism, and it gives a person a feeling of divinity and spirituality. It is a practice by which a person demarcates the separation of his soul from the outside world.

In Hinduism, applying *tilak* on the forehead has an impact on the person's personality as well. This *tilak* reflects the nature and personality of the person. Seen from a religious point of view, applying *tilak* increases the mental strength of a person and gives them spiritual energy.

THE SHAHI SNAN

Shahi Snan or 'royal bathing' by the saints associated with various *akhara*s on specific days is a major event of the Kumbh Mela. On these days, *sadhu*s associated with 14 *akhara*s participate in the ritual bath. Of these, 13 are registered *akhara*s or a monasteries for religious renunciates. They take baths according to their turn, a system said to be devised by the Britishers, which is still in vogue. After the seers take a bath and perform their rituals, millions of men and women who come from around the world, are allowed to take the holy dip. Shahi Snan of the Kumbh Mela is a very important event and every Hindu pilgrim wants to be a part of this occasion. During this period, faith moves like mountains on the bank of the river, and makes one endure the hardships which come as an integral part of the fair.

There is an interesting fact behind the marriage of 'Shahi' which is inherently Persian terminology, with a pious ritual of the Hindu religion— 'Snan'. The mingling of 'Shahi' with 'Snan' validates the cultural crossover and cross-pollination between languages which bred in medieval India, due to Arabic influences.

FACING PAGE: Purifying the soul through a holy dip in the sacred river

ABOVE: Dipping into faith and emerging with a renewed spirit

PAGES 132–133: A holy dip at the Sangam will wash away your burdens

Sacred religious texts and myths of India testify that in the carnal soul lives an eternal hope that things will be better, without the ever-imminent fear of them getting worse which cripples us here.

The Maha Kumbh represents a congregation of millions who gather to be freed from the vicious earthly cycle of life and death, and move towards a heavenly realm, where suffering or pain does not exist. An eternal life free of sins is the promise that comes attached to the magnificent event of Kumbh.

Pouring out *ghee* into the fire with a wooden ladle, the *sanyasi* should chant the following mantras:

Finding purity and peace with each sacred dip

Om: May the wind in all parts of myself, such as *pran* (life), *akuti* (feeling), intestines, throat, navel, and all other limbs be purified: I am a stainless, sinless light; this *ghee* is poured into the fire for my good. I bow to the wind within myself.

Om: the absolute *brahma* (or cause) is universal (or perfect), the *brahma* with attributes (or active *brahma*), also is universal. From the universal comes the universe. When we have abstracted the fullness of the perfect (or universal), the perfect (or universal) *brahma* is indeed left behind in our hearts.

—*Brihad-Aranyaka Upanishad*

The question of precedence in bathing on these occasions, formerly led to bloody fights. But the British governments, after inquiring into time-honoured practices, have laid down the following rules, which are strictly enforced by the Mela magistrate.

According to these rules, Naga *gosain*s take a bath first, then the Vaishnav Bairagi *sadhu*s, followed by the Udasin Nanak Panthi, and lastly the Nirmal *sadhu*s.

The Kumbh Mela of 1882 is thus described by Mr T Benson, I.C.S., in his report:

> To each corporation (Akhara) of religious ascetics was assigned a space of ground, within which it erected a temporary village or town for the accommodation of its members, in the centre of which moved the standards of the guild on a lofty flag staff. These encampments were orderly and

LEFT: The holy dip, a moment of cleansing and connection to the divine

well laid out, and of a comfortable description… The various camps formed were:

1. Nirvana Naga gosains
2. Niranjani, who was associated with the Juna
3. Bairagis, including three sects
4. Chhota Akhara Panchayati Udasin Nanak Panthis
5. Bara Akhara Panchayati with the Bandhua Akhara (Sikh)
6. Nirmal Sikh with Vrindavani

Here it is pertinent to mention that *akhara*s are given special preference during Shahi Snan as these *akhara*s played a pivotal role as the protectors of *dharma* while fighting against onslaught and invasion during the medieval period. Since Dharmayudha sacrifice and savageness are both manifested while slaying opponents, *akhara sadhu*s, are given special

LEFT: Female devotees going for the Shahi Snan

PAGES 138–139: *Sadhu*s from different *akhara*s decked in traditional regalia in a procession for the Shahi Snan.

treatment in Shahi Snan to wash away the sins that might have been committed by them during the elimination of the *vidharmi*.

The order in which the *akharas* take (Shahi Snan) is different for all four Kumbh Melas, and the main royal bath is separate for every Kumbh Mela. Shahi Snan is a ritual carried out with great faith and devotion by Hindu devotees. It is a symbolic ritual and has mythological significance.

The intergovernmental committee for the safeguarding of the intangible cultural heritage under UNESCO has included Kumbh Mela in the representative list of Intangible Cultural Heritage of Humanity at its 12th session held at Jeju, South Korea during 4–9 December, 2017.

The committee observed that 'Kumbh Mela' is the largest peaceful congregation of pilgrims on earth. The festival, held in Prayag, Haridwar, Ujjain and Nasik, is a synergetic set of rituals related to worship in India. It is a social ritual and festive event closely linked to the community's perception of its own history and memory. The element is compatible with existing human rights instruments since people from the walks of life, without any discrimination, participate in the festival with equal fervor. As a religious festival, the tolerance and inclusiveness that Kumbh Mela demonstrates is especially valuable for contemporary world.

FACING PAGE: An ascetic flaunts the fruits of his penance and devotion. The longer the locks, the longer duration of devotion they represent.

THE PILGRIMS

Pilgrims or worshipers flock to the Kumbh Mela by hundreds of thousands, not only to bathe in the sacred waters, but also to receive the blessings of the ascetics whom they have never seen elsewhere, in huge numbers. They press forward to glimpse the *babas* in the great Shahi Snan processions. Many pilgrims aspire for *darshan* of the holy ones. To see the *babas* up close, pilgrims may venture into the dense neighborhood of the *akharas*, to perhaps converse with them, or simply to have their silent blessing. As the dates of the Kumbh Mela approach, each of the

orders receives a formal invitation to the Mela from the government authorities in charge. The event is called Pravesh, or the 'Entrance,' and it begins when the *akharas* and their generals, the Mahamandaleshvars, make their processional entry into the Kumbh Mela grounds.

When devotees of Sanatan Dharma from all over the world gather at the banks of holy rivers Ganga, Shipra, and Godavari, in Prayag, Haridwar, Ujjain, and Nashik, then the mountain of faith rises to unearth the hidden seeker and philosopher within every person alive.

Devotees throng to the river bank. These include both monks, *sadhus*,

FACING PAGE: An ocean of faith and devotion at the confluence of rivers

saints, preachers, and *grahasth*s (householders). Prayag Kumbh is the largest in terms of the number of people participating, among all the four Kumbh Melas. It is attended by millions of people. In the ocean of humanity, all Indians, as well as a large number of devotees from foreign countries take a dip to realise faith and belief, in the world's biggest religious fair.

People from all walks of life irrespective of their nationality and creed present a kaleidoscopic atmosphere on the bank of holy rivers. Going by the *Guinness Book of World Records*, Prayag Kumbh is the biggest human confluence on the planet, and draws people from those not only within the country, but also from who scale miles to reach Mokshdayani Ganga.

Many researchers, who are infatuated by the spiritualistic aura of the holy city have recorded their thoughts about the Kumbh Mela.

RIGHT: Faith beyond boundaries, at the world's largest spiritual gathering

Some scholars from Harvard University have investigated Prayag Kumbh Mela, while Jack Hebner and David Osborn in *Kumbh Mela: The World's Act of Faith* said:

Pilgrims came by millions! Some arrived on overcrowded trains carrying five times the normal capacity. Some came by bus, some by car, some by ox-drawn carts and some rode on horses, camels and even elephants. The rich and famous chartered private planes and helicopters; the less affluent came on foot, carrying their bedrolls and camping equipment in heavy bundles on their heads. Wave after wave, the pilgrims formed a veritable river of humanity that flowed onto the banks of the Ganges at Prayag (Allahabad) to celebrate the greatest spiritual festival ever held – the Kumbh Mela.

LEFT: Foreign tourists and devotees taking in the spiritual aura

Devotees of different nationalities—joy in every heart, faith in every step

They further said:

On this occasion, pilgrims from every nook and corner of India – speaking different languages and dialects, wearing distinctive markings on their foreheads, and donning various types of dress and observing different manners and customs and yes, sporting untiring smiles – meet together for a holy bath in sacred waters.

In Prayag, apart from Kumbh Mela, Magh Mela is organised every year in the month of January and February.

Millions of worshipers gather at the confluence of the Ganges, Yamuna, and (now dry) Saraswati rivers, to celebrate Hindu faith. Every year, for one lunar cycle, a vast tent city grows up on the floodplain. Roads appear, bridges and steel plates are built over the river, residential camps are marked out, and the more celebrated religious organisations pitch huge marquees. Besides, all daily facilities required by the pilgrims are available. The Magh Mela is a colossal affair. In the 12th year, the size of the faithful in the Kumbh Mela inflates to an unimaginable number at the mystic confluence of three sacred rivers.

Those who reside in tents during Magh Mela are called *kalpwasis*. They are mostly folks from villages, the elderly, and of the privileged castes. Their aim is to attain religious merit by attending for 12 consecutive years. They seek to renounce all worldly ways and everyday comforts, in order to start living a purely spiritual existence.

The word *kalpwasi* is made of two words. These are *kalpa*, denoting the transformation of the self through inner resolve, and *vas*, denoting the living out of this resolve.

In general, the *kalpwasi*s live in encampments based on where they come from, and are organised by *panda*s. The camps are little more than rows of tents. They bring their own bedding, furniture and supplies. People sleep on the ground, wrapped in blankets. *Kalpwasi*s eat meals at one time and their foods are very simple, and without any spices.

The day of *kalpwasi*s starts very early and bathing in the Ganga is the most important part of their rituals. They take a bath and perform *puja* to holy river morning and evening.

British universities and the University of Allahabad came together for their research about the Kumbh and Magh Melas. They say:

Many different people can be found at the Mela. There are the day bathers who do not stay in the

ABOVE: *Kalpwasi*s going about their daily activities—a scene of faith, spirituality, and humanity

PAGES 152–153: Countless lights illuminating the air of spiritual trepidation and peace

Mela but who visit, especially on the more auspicious days of the lunar calendar, to the bathe in the Ganges. There are those who serve the Mela, sweeping, removing rubbish, cleaning latrines and a myriad of other tasks. There are shopkeepers, social activists, police officers and fire fighters. But at the core of the event are the pilgrims or Kalpwasis who live in tented encampments for the entire month.

Pilgrims who attend the Kumbh Mela are overwhelmingly elderly people, a large number of whom are *sadhus*. It is truly one of the most spectacular religious gatherings in the world.

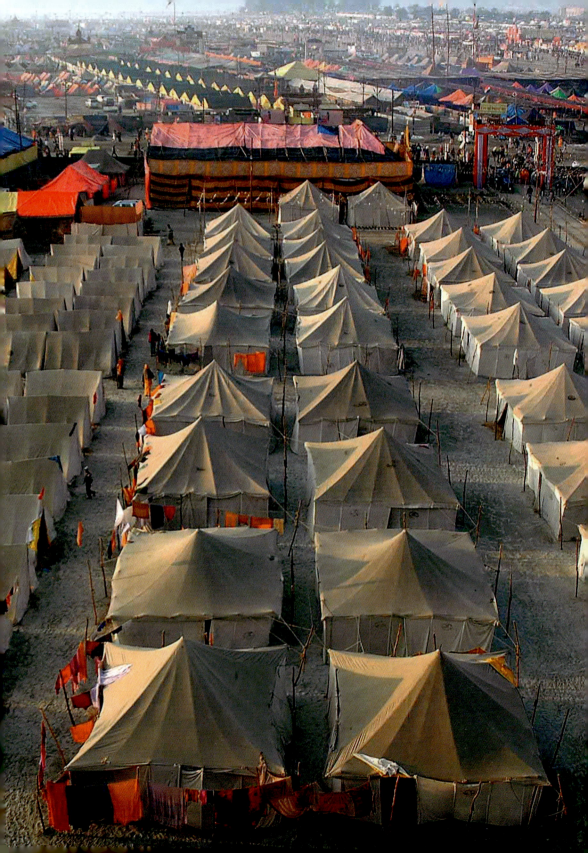

CITY OF TENTS

A colourful, sprawling, tented city springs up beside the holy river during the Kumbh Melas of Prayag, Haridwar, Ujjain and Nasik. During the Kumbh Mela, private companies set up luxury tents, and state tourism corporations also set up tent cities at Kumbh Mela, which fit every budget. The township is sustained by an entirely local economy.

In comparison to the Haridwar, Ujjain and Nasik, Kumbh Melas, Prayag Kumbh covers the largest area. In Allahabad, now Prayagraj, the Kumbh area is usually divided into three parts to create the required infrastructure for the Kumbh Mela tent city.

The first one is around the Sangam area, where there is a huge tract of open land, including the parade ground which belongs to the army, the second is the river Ganga toward Jhunsi, and the third, across the Yamuna, towards a suburban area of Prayag, known as Arail.

Since river water separates these areas, floating pontoon bridges are erected to connect them. In view of administrative convenience, the Prayag Kumbh Mela of 2013 was divided into 14 sectors and it was set up on 1,936 hectares of land. Whereas, the Prayag Ardh Kumbh

FACING PAGE: The tent city of Kumbh, where worshippers are united by faith

Mela in 2019, was divided into 20 sectors and it was spread over an area of about 3,200 hectares. This could be compared with the 2016 Simhastha Kumbh in Ujjain, where the total area of the tent city was 3,061 hectares whereas in 2004, Simhastha Kumbh was spread over 2154.42 hectares and the Ujjain Kumbh Mela was divided into 22 sectors. The government spent Rs 3183.61 for the Kumbh Mela and other development work in Ujjain.

But worshipers remember Prayag Ardh Kumbh Mela in 2019 for the reason that many facilities that were set up for the first time in the history of Kumbh Mela. This included approximately 20,000 dustbins, 140 tippers, 40 compactors for solid waste management, shuttle bus, e-rickshaws and CNG-run auto rickshaws.

Apart from these, over 40,000 LED lights, laser shows, facade lighting, food courts, integrated command and control centres, and more than 1000 CCTV cameras were used, and

RIGHT: Aerial view of the meticulously organised temporary tent shelters in the Mela

The facade of a tent enterance in the Mela area

delegates from 70 countries visited the Prayag Ardh Kumbh Mela.

During the 2001 Kumbh, Jal Nigam, the state's water authority, laid 350 km of pipelines, in addition to setting up 15,000 taps for the water supply. For the drainage of waste-water, *kaccha* drains had to be dug below every tap.

On the trunk supply line, provision was made for 1,100 fire hydrants.

To quench the thirst of pilgrims, 12,000 drinking water taps were set up along the roads. Electric substations were installed to maintain a continuous supply of electricity to the Mela tent city, in the cold month of January.

All the facilities of any modern city are available in the tent city at Kumbh Mela.

The health department provided the Mela area with medical and sanitation facilities, and ensured regular cleaning and sweeping. The supply of food grains, edible oils, fire wood, cooking gas, kerosene oil, vegetables, and fruits, was streamlined. Restaurants, tea stalls, and sweet shops came up.

In 2001, for the first time in the history of the Kumbh, 14 market complexes were opened, with six government fair price shops, a grocery, two shops for edible oils and items of daily use, two vegetable and fruit shops, as well as outlets for firewood and kerosene oil.

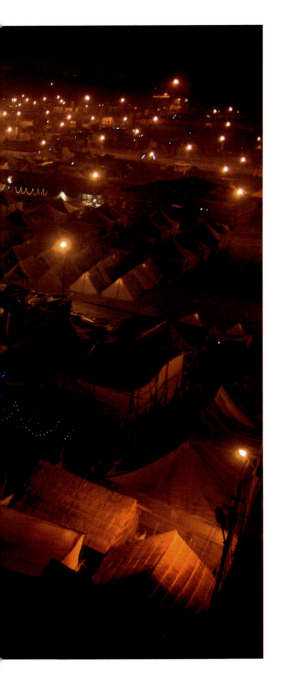

About 20 kiosks and two cyber cafes were also setup; they were especially handy for many reporters who came to cover the Kumbh.

Many ashrams and institutions like Ramakrishna Mission and the Bharat Seva Ashram, set up camps in the Kumbh Mela area for worshipers. These institutions ensured the availability of all the basic comforts. They also distribute blankets, organise health check-ups, feed the needy, and conduct evening prayers and meditation sessions.

Followers of Kabir Panth, who do not advocate the idea practicing of penance, too joined, and came under the blanket of Kumbh by erecting their pandal or tents.

Megasthenes, the Greek ambassador to the court of Chandragupta Maurya, who visited

LEFT: The night view of the tent city at Kumbh Mela is a mesmerising sight, with rows of illuminated tents stretching across the horizon, glowing under the night sky.

PAGES 162–163: The vast tent city, where pilgrims find refuge and unity at Kumbh Mela.

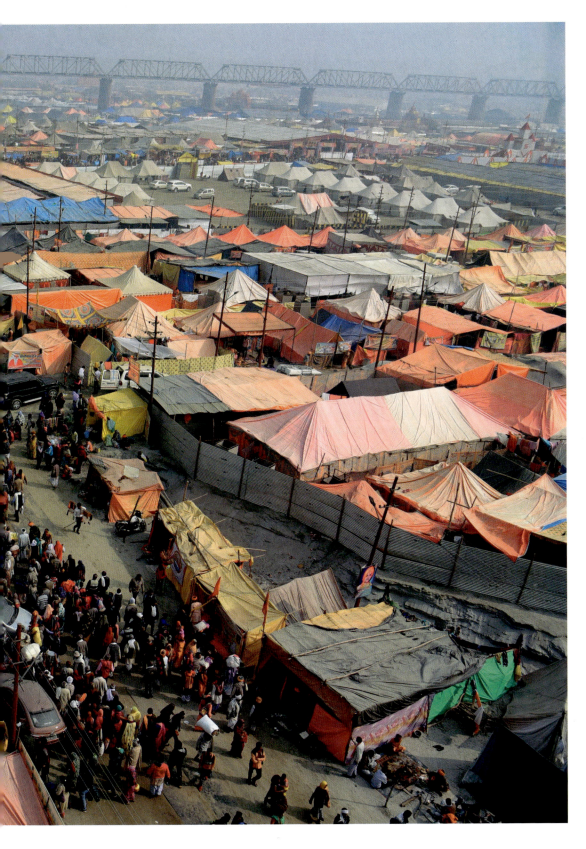

ABOVE: The night view of the tent city at Kumbh Mela.

PAGES 164–165: A unique gathering of religion, faith and philosophy at midnight at Prayag Kumbh.

in the 4th century BCE, was amazed to see a city of tents. A Harvard University study said, 'The four Mela cities are urban areas that are structured by their water bodies. Allahabad is situated at the fork of the confluence between the Ganga and Yamuna, whereas Haridwar, Nashik, and Ujjain have linear organizations, usually along one of their respective rivers.'

In a few instances, the cities spill over to the opposite bank, using foot and car bridges to join the two sides. The riverfront and bathing access is central to the Mela in these cities. The transport infrastructure of roads, trains, and highways is critical to the smooth functioning of Mela, and these great pilgrimage fairs provide the occasion for a concerted effort to improve the transportation infrastructure… The urban layout of each city also must include the space for the large temporary encampments that are essential for the Mela.

The city, therefore, interacts with an unpopulated terrain nearby, used alternately for agriculture and as a site for the temporary city during the Mela. This is the fertility and dynamism of the temporary city as well as the long stretches of relatively quiet agricultural landscapes in between.'

The grid system was first used by the colonial government in the mid-19th century to build the City of Tents.

Tents for sleeping, eating, religious gatherings, entertainment, and socialising make up the basic spatial character of the Kumbh Mela city. The Mela area is zoned from one grid block to the next, so that residential and public spaces are distinct, interspersed with hospitals, eating areas, firework departments, police stations, railway reservation centres, media centres, public toilets, pontoon bridges, etc.

Michael Wood, a famous British documentary maker, who has done a series on the history of India, says that each tent in the fair area has its own address.

Jawaharlal Nehru in his book *Discovery of India*, averred:

In my own city of Allahabad, or Haridwar, I would go to the great bathing festivals, the Kumbh Mela, and see hundreds of thousands of people come, as their forebears had come for thousands of years from all over India, to bathe in the Ganges. I would remember descriptions of these festivals written thirteen hundred years ago by Chinese pilgrims and others, and even then these festivals were ancient and lost in an unknown antiquity. What was the tremendous faith, I wondered, that had drawn our people for untold generations to this famous river of India?' (1946; 199: 51)

NEW ERA
OF KUMBH

In the era of change and commotion, where archaic and primitive tradition falls apart, the Kumbh is also not an exception. We encounter dazzling changes in the 21st century, of the Sanatan tradition, which become quite evident during the Kumbh and Ardh Kumbh Mela, organised in the first half of this century.

*Akhara*s which draw the maximum attention of devotees, were chiefly formed to protect Sanatan dharma. During the Prayag Ardh Kumbh 2019, Juna Akhara, one of the major Akharas of Naga *sadhu*s, gave invitations to Dalit

women while Dalit and Mahadalit men were also given the title of saints. It is pertinent to mention that the Akhara is believed to have been founded in 904 CE in Mandavi, Gujarat.

After Juna, Niranjani is believed to be the second largest *akhara*. Niranjani Akhara also consecrates a 52 foot high holy flag in their camp in the Kumbh and Maha Kumbh Melas. The number 52 symbolises the 52 houses of seers to which the Shaivite *akhara*s belong. Before Mouni Amavasya, Dalit women were initiated by saints, and among them a few women saints were also made Mahamandaleshwar.

This is the first time in the history of Juna Akhara that such a large

FACING PAGE: Seeking divinity in the lap of the holy confluence of sacred rivers

number of Dalit women were made saints. Juna Akhara is one of the 13 major *akhara*s of Naga *sadhu*s. According to the Akhara, there are millions of saints within their fold. Of these, the number of Dalit and Mahadalit women is around 500.

At present, eight have been given the title of Mahamandaleshwar, of which five are male and three are female. The Kinnar Akhara (akhara of eunuchs) showed their presence on this auspicious occasion, and set up their base camps ushering a new era of inclusive spiritualism.

On the other side, Sadhvi Pragya Thakur, a fire brand leader-established a new *akhara* called the Bharat Bhakti Akhara, at Prayag Ardh Kumbh. She also announced herself as the first Acharya Maha Mandaleshwar and the head of the Akhara. Her Pattabhishek (coronation) ceremony was performed by members of the Akhil Bharatiya Kashi Vidhyat Parishad and some

LEFT: Bridging cultures—foreign devotees finding unity in diversity at Kumbh Mela

Foreign devotees embracing the spirit of Kumbh Mela

seers. The ceremony took place at Divya Prem Seva Mission, located on the Kumbh Mela campus, on the occasion of Maghi Purnima.

Sadhvi Pragya was earlier a member of the Juna Akhara and would now be known as Acharya Maha Mandaleshwar Purnchetan Anand Giri.

As of now, the Akhara has not been recognised by the Akhil Bhartiya Akhara Parishad, the apex body of the 13 *akhara*s of the country. Pragya Thakur says:

I have established the Akhara for the protection of Sanatan

A global gathering and journey of faith

dharma, which I would be doing along with all the seers of different Akharas. All seers and devotees are welcome to join this new Akhara which would be a separate entity and does not want recognition from the ABAP.

Then President of the Akhil Bhartiya Akhara Parishad (ABAP), Swami Narendra Giri said:

Establishing a new Akhara has now become a fashion. We would welcome her if she decides to come under the umbrella of the thirteen established Akharas as was done by the Kinnar Akhara, but there is no question of recognizing her new Akhara by the Akhara Parishad.

The chief patron of Juna Akhara, Mahant Hari Giri said:

India is an independent country and everyone is free to establish an Akhara. There are around 5,500 Akharas and around 568 political parties, and this becomes an additional one.

In 2013, breaking age old tradition, a group of women seers announced the formation of the first all-women Akhara Shri Sarveshwar Maha Deo Vaikunthdham Muktidwar Akhara Pari or Pari Akhara, at the Prayag Kumbh Mela Magh Mela on the bank of Sangam. However, at the Nashik Kumbh the next year, women were denied a place on dais and

RIGHT: Female empowerment exemplified by the creation of Pari Akhara

Foreign devotees connecting with ancient traditions

refused a separate time slot for the Shahi Snan.

The original 13 *akhara*s are said to be established by Adi Shankaracharya and all are male-dominated. Around 100 saffron-clad women came from different districts of Uttar Pradesh and marched under the banner of Shankaracharya Sadguru Trikal Bhawante Shree Sarveshwer Mahadeo from Mahvir Marg to Sangam. At the banks of the Ganga, they performed Ganga Pujan and other rituals that included *abhishek* and *aarti*.

The 2016 Ujjain Simhastha Kumbh Mela was very special in the history of Kumbh History for the formation of the Kinnar Akhara.

Maha Mandaleshwar Laxminarayan Tirpathi is the head of Kinnar Akhara. A day before the Simhastha Kumbh, a procession by the Kinnar Akhara was taken out of the Dussehra Ground in Ujjain. It was received by Kinnar Laxaminarayan Tirpathi and Sanatan guru Ajay Das.

It was a matter of great pride for the Kinnar Akhara for the first time to join the Ujjain Kumbh and they attribute this to Sanatan Guru Ajay Das. The Peshwai (procession) was a grand event of power show. Many eunuchs of the country including Peeteshwar and Uppeetheshwar of the Kinnar Akhara participated in this procession, with the tricolour flag on their e-rickshaw.

The ABAP, an organisation of 13 major *akhara*s, had earlier refused to recognise the Kinnar Akhara. In spite of the protest, the Kinnar Akhara participated in Simhastha Kumbh saying that they do not need any recognition in the city of Shiva.

Laxmi says that society has long ignored the existence of eunuchs; they have established this Akhara to get back their lost existence and to provide a respectable place for eunuchs in society.

At the Prayag Ardh Kumbh in 2019, carpets were rolled out for a total of 13 *akhara*s, who were the integral members. Out of these, seven were Shaivites, three Vaishnavas, and three Sikh. This Ardh Kumbh witnessed the Peshwai of the Kinnar Akhara for the first time. All these *akhara*s have their own specialities and importance. Their laws are different, as are their routines and their presiding deities.

Saint Kabir, a great opponent of religious rituals, kept questioning the existence of the Hindu *bhagwan* and Muslim *khuda* by firing salvoes at the methods of worship of both Hindus and Muslims. But the Kabirpanthi followers also participate in the Kumbh Mela.

Modern Times:

The city of tents is metamorphosing into the citadel of cosy swish cottages, escorted and equipped with modern IT gadgets and sophisticated utilities.

*Sadhu*s, who once believed in containment, are now basking under modernisation. Sporting high-end phones and saddling motorcades of lavish vehicles, godmen, who are

History was created by the establishment of the Kinnar Akhara in Ujjain Simhastha

trusted to have a direct connection with god are no longer hesitant to explore the power of fibre optics to smoothen the path of eternity.

Though Allahabad (now Prayagraj) continues to be a witness to the biggest congregation on the planet, distances are impediments no longer. With many ritual practitioners treading on the chariots of the information technology revolution, now pilgrims from all nooks and corners of the globe can witness, watch, and virtually immerse themselves in the sea of devotion.

'Now devotees, who could not pay a visit to Kumbh, can virtually participate through dedicated and customised online packages including *puja*, offerings, and others,' said a pundit while showcasing the versatility of his website, and thus creating *dharma* in a new avatar.